ERODE WITH ME

Nikki Dudley is managing editor of streetcake magazine and also runs the streetcake writing prize. She has collections and pamphlets out with: Knives Forks and Spoons, Beir Bua, Hem Press, and now Sídhe Press. She won the Virginia Prize 2020 and her second novel, *Volta* was published in May 2021. She works in marketing for charities by day and has a (not so secret) love for karaoke and netball.

Also by Nikki Dudley

Just One More Before I Go   (Sídhe Press, 2023)

Exorcism Becomes Habit   (Hem Press, 2023)

Volta   (Aurora Metro Books, 2021)

Fanny B. Mine   (Beir Bua Press, 2021)

Hope Alt Delete   (Knives Forks and Spoons, 2016)

Ellipsis   (Sparkling Books, 2010)

exits/origins   (Knives Forks and Spoons, 2010)

Contents

[STOP]   7

[THE GAPING HOLE]   8

[HOW SHE GOT MADE]   9

[I SEND MY APOLOGIES]   10

[SAMPLE DIALOGUES]   12

[FOR MY SWEETHEART, NO MORE]   13

[YEAH, NETTLES]   14

[INSTRUCTIONS FOR DISASSEMBLY]   15

[SEE ME]   18

[THIS IS WHERE YOU FIND ME]   19

[JARRING]   20

[EXAM SITUATIONS]   21

[TIME TRAVEL]   23

[THE FINE PRINT]   24

[ERODE WITH ME]   25

[ENDINGS]   27

[NOTES]   29

[ACKNOWLEDGEMENTS]   31

ISBN: 978-1-916938-00-7

Cover designed by Stuart McPherson & Aaron Kent

Edited and Typeset by Aaron Kent

Broken Sleep Books Ltd
Rhydwen
Talgarreg
Ceredigion
SA44 4HB

Broken Sleep Books Ltd
Fair View
St Georges Road
Cornwall
PL26 7YH

Erode with Me

Nikki Dudley

Broken Sleep Books

[STOP]

The nights ----- I dream
the best
are the nights I
                    dream of
                            being shot.

Structure can be
[sus   pect]?
                        Note: /// I feel blank inside.

            I call you   *via*

                            ALL/WAYS
                                    [just here]

                Argue/ Brief words hold

                                    up the
                                    sides
                                    of you!*

                    (*please stop pretending)

[THE GAPING HOLE]

WHERE?

this pen
finally undressed

a mythic quality / shivers

newborn
thoughts

/ / / / / / / evolving

if

nightmares find a key.

A caterpillar uncurling,

metamorphosis

eloping secrecy.

*Sometimes
I just want to
live
in a field.*

Visions creep

via

harmony,
shunned

the gaping whole

of me

the

[HOW SHE GOT MADE]

I remember being afraid of AN ENSEMBLE TO DIE FOR so I would pull my covers up AGAINST ERGONOMICS.

I remember cracking THE MAYHEM FACTORY on the floor at swimming and not knowing THE LORDS OF DISCIPLINE.

I remember WRITING A SLASHER-MOVIE SEQUEL in a cupboard with my brother for hours until our mum thought we were lost.

I remember making A DICKENS OF A TASK with my brothers and daring THE ANATOMY OF A FROG.

I UNLEASHED THE GOBLINS in the night but AFTER SAYING GOODBYE we got caught. (Every time).

I remember when THE HEART let me hold YOUR OWN INCOMPETENCE!

[I SEND MY APOLOGIES]

I sliced my fingers open

Once on THE STREETS

OF A FOREIGN COUNTRY.

Now I KNOW BETTER.

I LOVE YOU,

Once I USED TO BE PRETTY, believed vampires would bite

me - *I MISS YOU, I*

Now I have nightmares I AM UNABLE TO SHARE MY SECRET about not

being able to *WANT YOU, I*

NEED YOU in my

sleep. save you.

Once my dad told me I *NEVER LIKED POETRY?*

Now I think about Keats (standing on the shore alone)

thinking I'M AFRAID OF WOMEN WHO WEAR CAPRI

PANTS!

Once I counted net / / /

morf

kcab

and

STOLE YOUR DUCK*.

Now my mouth WEIGHS OVER

A £ AND A HALF.

(ALWAYS WANTED TO ROB A
BANK covered in mud.)

*Yes, it
Now I remember I COUNLDN'T CRY when I   was me
walked into the room.

Sorry

Once. Once. Once. I held ALL THE BLUEBERRIES as you

took your

last breath

...I WAS DRIVING   *TOO FAST*.

[SAMPLE DIALOGUES]

A different way of asking
                    CLOSED/OPEN
It sounds like you're stuck - powerful questions tend to
stop people.
          WHY DON'T YOU CARE?

A narrow tunnel that usually leads to inside / out.
A rope is called an anchor,
          to the edge of improbability.

                              NOTE: there are times when *alive* will be
                                    very dramatic and times when it will be
                                                          very quiet.

You see a historical pattern of trouble. Where do you
abandon yourself?
At the same time, it's worth celebrating when this happens.
/////////////////////////////Disconnecting?   *Say so.*

[FOR MY SWEETHEART, NO MORE]

lies / lie / lied / lying
----- ----- ~~with me~~

                            the waves
say nothing say nothing   build the waves
        under your breath   swell
                            the waves   tra
                            the waves   ces
        the drunk   the   of
                                    ha ha ha
                                    ha   poi
                                  ha ha ha   son
                              ha ha ha
                            ha ha ha ha ha ha hu
        ha ha ha ha ha ha ha ha ha ha ha ha ha ha
        ha ha ha ha ha ha ha ha ha ha ha ha ha ha
ha ha ha ha ha ha ha ha ha ha ha ha ha ha ha ha ha
ha ha ha ha ha ha ha ha ha ha ha ha ha ha ha ha ha
        ha ha ha ha ha ha ha ha ha ha ha ha ha ha
            ha ha ha ha ha ha ha ha ha ha ha ha ha ha ha haa
    ha ha ha ha ha ha ha ha ha ha ha ha ha ha ha ha ha ha

[YEAH, NETTLES]

But what   age?
Spoiled, drifted, purred. The smothering
of birth.

Hi wish.

                        Be dreams, be waves, wash things.

Yeah, nettles, love
        missed and lied. Cold
body kept and fried. He's still

                              landing.

        Wander / lie / sigh –
        doubt.

[INSTRUCTIONS FOR DISASSEMBLY]

REMOVE PART A FROM PART B

My family is a building site. We can slide from

top to bottom in

10 seconds
to avoid all those
messy

in-between floors.

Problem 1: Those in-between floors need building too.

INSERT PART C INTO PART F

In our house, someone left the sand out and it rained. Now
the sand covers everything. It's like egg shells that settle
in every corner, under every nail.

**Problem 2: Sand is hard to shake off, it
drags you back, a dry hole refilling
over and over and over**

CONNECT SCREW 7 TO PART G

People kept moving the floorboards and

I got   hurt so
                 many times
                 I stopped
     walking around   the house.

Now, when I visit, I am a surveyor
          trying to add them together.

Problem 3: The count is wrong or
I am?

AFFIX SCREW 5 INTO PARTS A AND C

I know how our room was built but not how to keep it together.
When we built it, angles made sense but
the walls kept moving and the doors
don't lead where I knew
in another time   Do not leave children unattended
another

Problem 4: My mind wanders in our past
and now I smell warning gas.

ATTACH PART H TO PART E

When a house subsides, it happens millimetre by millimetre
and I'm holding it up like a leaning tower
and the love explodes like lava
when the pipes fracture
and the memories are irremovable plasters
layers upon layers upon lay here / with me /
and remember how the sky was clear
and blue and we smashed that wall
like Lego

Problem 5: Breaking the walls left us saturated in dust.

INSERT PART... SOMETHING... SOMEWHERE

I learned love from a cement mixer.
It turns and twists and hardens if you let it rest.
The scraping sound of spreading cement echoes
in my ears, the way bricks fit together and if they don't,
you break them.

Problem 6: I didn't fit. I'm sorry.

INSERT SCREW 279 INTO ANOTHER HOLE WE FOUND

You can still love a house if
the roof tiles are missing and things leak in
the walls are warping from the flood
the floorboards can't hold the pressure and they're flammable
and smoke rises because voices battle like a forest fire doesn't care
for trees.

**Problem 7: I thought erasure would be silence
but building a new house
is a set of controlled implosions,
rebuilding a heart
without an architectural drawing.**

...CAN ANYONE SEE THE INSTRUCTIONS?

Problem 8: I make mistakes.

[SEE ME]

Impenetrable. A bouncer

to searching fingers crossing   brink.

Muscles.   Tense.

An avalanche threatening release,

                        an   obstacle

                                    that quickly

                                                becomes

                                                            a trap

[THIS IS WHERE YOU FIND ME]

Maybe ▮▮▮ an SOS ▮▮▮▮▮▮
▮▮▮▮ bring egg fried rice ▮▮▮
▮▮▮▮▮▮ read the signs ▮▮
▮▮▮▮▮ reflectors ▮▮ It kissed me
▮▮▮▮▮ fucked me twice as hard.

Blank. ▮▮▮▮▮ we all crash? ▮
▮ be in my space ▮▮ the lines ▮▮
space ▮ air ▮▮ I wish ▮▮▮ I should
▮▮▮▮▮▮

My body is ▮▮▮ the asphalt ▮
▮ forgotten ice cream. ▮▮▮
▮▮▮▮ shaped cold spot
▮▮▮▮▮
▮▮ still shouting ▮▮

▮ Road, ▮▮▮▮ you
understand, ▮▮▮▮ That spot ▮
▮▮▮▮▮
▮▮▮▮ That date
▮▮ This patch ▮▮
▮▮

▮▮ who hadn't thought about ending a life?

[JARRING]

I was beginning ~~to feel~~. Thought I'd
mastered it. But we learn, we never
master a thing.

Ice cracking   that swipe of metal

sprays of blood

jarring

cold burning

outst
retch
ed
finge
rs.

I wouldn't allow myself

to
fall.

[EXAM SITUATIONS]

The next morning, I went back alone

pages out pages out do not

write your name before out pages

out damn

pages

I cannot possibly describe to you how I emit blood in exam situations.

Note: BIRDS HAVE ALMOST NO SENSE OF SMELL.
  -Where is the exit?

I forgot the word

and now I can't

There was a fearful silence.

Absolutely motionless, out on the main road. Something is coming.

Every word transforms

[THIS POEM]

This poem started like this and went on like that then became the
something else when the end of the sentence came and things end
of the
just fell down like that and then I went round and round sente
Y like
o and round and round and nce
u then someone said came
something went
w on
over there about eggs? How they hatch but then it was chocolate
er
and nothing made sense until

I turned around and saw the trees outside and they were budding
m
and things were moving
is
and nothing stopped -
in
fo like this and
what did you ask
r
me? like that
m
ed fell
And what the hell am I writing anyway? This isn't a poem is it? I
down
am afraid you were misinformed and I take it back and what did
like that
you ask me?

I answered like this and like that and the poem said nothing
the trees
back because maybe that's not its name after all and I need a

dictionary but the words the trees
won't stay

in line outside and

they were
budding

[TIME TRAVEL]

From the fierce &
wonderful, ARE WE MOST PRODUCTIVE?

(Follow me here)

Some sort of narrative? I can feel -
THE COLD EARTH - far from those I loved.

He asks 200 years ago - 'how long will this posthumous existence
of mine last?'

I hold it towards him. IT'S TIME
I GOT ON WITH IT.

A fresh spinning of a story -
            what a set of people
                        we live amongst.

[THE FINE PRINT]

I am committed ███████████████████████████ ██████
██████████████████████████████████

██████████████ in full ██████████████
███████████████████████████████████
██
We accept ███████████████████████

████████████████████████████████████
██████████████████

████████████████████████████████████
██████████████ the decision ██████████
██████████████ approximately ██████████
████████████████████████████████████
████████████████ If you are intending to
████████████████████████████████
██████████████████ avoid ██████████
████████████

████████████████████████████████████
████████████████████████████████████
████████████████████████████████████
██████████████ control, please note ████████
██████████████ you do not have ██████ rights ██████
████████████████████████████

[ERODE WITH ME]

I re:

mind

live

member -

    a)   friends across a table / different grains

    b)   impending rain / the heavy cardboard smell

    c)   the hardness of glass / invisible fingerprints

    d)   the ground beneath me / connected to mud, roots

    e)   holding hands / being unseen.

I for:

get

go

gone -

    a)   Mum's hands / the smell of her make up lingering

    b)   night smothering day / quiet assassin

    c)   unknown voices / moving in between

    d)   no invisible threads / walking without trace.

Faces are sharper on screen than in memory.

(((Who are you? Who's talking?

              Where's your face? HEAR ME. SEE ME.

We break up,

and down, and a part. You jump

when you talk. When you t-a-l-k   YOU JUMP.

A cliff crumbles with time.

Dear love,
What if the pieces make nothing?

Erode with me, lie with me, crumple

in my arms
and feel
the wait of
the world.

[ENDINGS]

TODAY

Yesterday I lay ASLEEP in bed and DREAMED about ENDINGS.

Today I can't SHUT my eyes.

IS TODAY

Yesterday the GROUND was EMPTY of BRIGHTNESS.

TODAY?

Today the sky is GRASS FROZEN in the SUN.

TODAY

Yesterday I FORGET INCONSTANCE with ANTAGONISTS.

TODAY IS

Today I VISUALISED

STAYING.

[NOTES]

HOW SHE GOT MADE uses found material from Empire film magazine.

YEAH, NETTLES was created with a homolinguistic translation of 'Wish' by Carol Ann Duffy, followed by a redaction and re-translation.

EXAM SITUATIONS contains some found material from Danny, the Champion of the World by Roald Dahl.

FIERCE AND WONDERFUL has some found material from using the hashtag #KeatsTweets on Twitter.

SAMPLE DIALOGUES is found material from Co-Active Coaching by Henry Kimsey-House, Karen Kimsey-House, Phillip Sandahl and Laura Whitworth (Nicholas Brealey Publishing, 2018)

I SEND MY APOLOGIES uses found material from the Post Secret book.

ENDINGS is an antonym translation of a poem I wrote.

[ACKNOWLEDGEMENTS]

Thank you to JP Seabright, Richard Capener and Emma Filtness for providing feedback on this manuscript. Thanks to Aaron Kent and the Broken Sleep team for believing in my work. Thanks also to the MumWrite sessions, where some of these works were born.

Thanks, as always, to Joe.

Thanks to these publications for featuring these poems in one form or another: Selcouth Station, -algia and Untitled Writing.

LAY OUT YOUR UNREST

www.ingramcontent.com/pod-product-compliance
Lightning Source LLC
Chambersburg PA
CBHW021948040426
42448CB00008B/1296